Your Mind Matters

Beating STRESS AND ANXIETY

Honor Head

W
FRANKLIN WATTS
LONDON • SYDNEY

First published in Great Britain in 2019
by The Watts Publishing Group
10 9 8 7 6 5 4 3 2 1
All rights reserved

Editor: Nicola Edwards
Cover design: Lisa Peacock and Thy Bui
Inside design: Matthew Lilly
Cover and inside illustrations
by Roberta Terracchio
Consultant: Diana Cant, Child and Adolescent Psychotherapist
and member of Tavistock Psychotherapists

ISBN 978 1 4451 6451 9 (HB); 978 1 4451 6452 6 (PB)
Printed in China

FSC
www.fsc.org
MIX
Paper from
responsible sources
FSC® C104740

Franklin Watts
An imprint of
Hachette Children's Group
Part of the Watts Publishing Group
Carmelite House
50 Victoria Embankment
London EC4Y 0DZ
An Hachette UK Company
www.hachette.co.uk
www.franklinwatts.co.uk

WHAT IS A TRUSTED ADULT?

Throughout the book we suggest you speak to a trusted adult. This is a person who makes you feel safe and that you can trust. It could be a parent or carer or another family member, such as an aunt or uncle or grandparent. It could be a teacher or someone you know well, such as a family friend or a friend's parent or carer. Or it could be someone at the end of a helpline (see pages 46-47).

CONTENTS

WHAT IS STRESS?

Everybody experiences stress throughout their lifetime. Normal stress can sometimes be a good thing.

DESCRIBING STRESS

Stress is the feeling you get when you're worried, upset or uncomfortable about something. Stress affects you mentally and physically. It can make you feel sick, make your heart pound, give you a headache and make it difficult to sleep properly. You may feel like going to the loo all the time, start shivering or sweating or feel like your legs have turned to jelly.

NORMAL STRESS

We usually feel stressed or worried when something new or important is about to happen, such as starting a new school, taking an exam, trying out a new hobby or making a presentation in front of the class. These feelings are perfectly normal and shouldn't last very long. This kind of stress can help you to focus on what you are doing. It can make you work harder to get your homework done on time or give you the energy to play a better game of football.

BAD STRESS

If you feel stressed all the time, can't sleep or eat because you are worrying, can't concentrate at school, feel irritable and grumpy and shout at people when you don't mean to, these can be signs that you are badly stressed or are staying stressed for long periods of time.

This kind of bad stress can be caused by a traumatic event such as the death of a loved one or a family breaking up. But it can also be caused by something like constantly worrying over how many likes we have or the comments we're getting on social media. Instead of the stress helping us and then going away, it builds up and can make us feel worse physically and mentally.

TRY THIS!

Look out for these boxes throughout this book. They will give you hints and tips on quick ways to improve your emotional and physical health that you can try every day or whenever you need to.

STRESS TEST

No one should feel
stressed all the time.
Think about how stressed
you are and why.

BUSY LIVES

Young people have a lot going on in their lives.
Exams, schoolwork, making friends, family life, social
media … it can be great fun and exciting, but it can be
stressful at times, too. Many young people look after a
parent or sibling who isn't well, or have to cope with a
family splitting up. Life for adults can also be stressful
and this can affect the whole family. When we feel
stressed our brain releases hormones into our body to
help cope with the event. If the stress goes on for
too long, our body is constantly flooded with
these hormones and this can damage
our health physically and mentally.

STOP AND THINK

How do you feel right now? If you feel relaxed that's fine, but if you're feeling tense, worrying about what's going to happen after class or after school, have thoughts going round and round in your head and a funny feeling in your tummy, you could be feeling very stressed.

WHY STRESSED?

When you feel stressed, stop and take a few breaths and think about why you feel stressed. If there is one specific thing worrying you, visualise or create a picture in your mind of everything going to plan and ending well. If you can't pinpoint one thing, or there are loads of things, take some time to try and stop the cycle of stress instead of carrying on worrying about it all. Too much stress can affect your health and your schoolwork and make you feel miserable.

> " *I heard Mum and Dad talking about money problems. It made me worry that we would have to move house and I would have to find a new school and I'd lose all my friends. I couldn't think of anything else but I didn't want Mum and Dad to know I'd heard. Eventually I told my aunt and she told my parents. They did have some money problems but nothing like as bad as I imagined. I was worrying for nothing!*
>
> Ben, 12 "

COPING WITH STRESS

There are lots of different
ways to cope with stress.
First you have to know what's
causing the stress.

TAKE ACTION

If the thing that's making you stressed is something
obvious, like an exam or giving a class talk, you can take
steps to deal with your stress. Prepare for the event.
Do the work required, whether it's practising
a talk, researching a subject or
revising. Make a list of what
needs to be done and organise
your time so you get everything
done in time and feel that you
have control over the event,
rather than it having you in a
grip of worry. Accept that if it
does go wrong, it's not the end
of the world, but feel confident
that it will all go to plan.

SOCIAL MEDIA

We spend a lot of time on social media posting images, commenting and keeping up with our online and real friends. It can be fun but it can also cause stress and worry if we don't get enough likes or shares, or the right sort of comments. We might worry about not being online to accept an invite straightaway, or stress about missing out on something cool that is happening. Social media life can begin to take over, and instead of being fun, becomes a big source of stress.

If this is happening, think about what is making you stressed. Is it not getting enough likes or shares? Why does this stress you? Think about why you need the approval of others. Is it to boost your self-esteem or because of FOMO – fear of missing out?

TRY THIS!

If social media is stressing you out you can decide to have a social media de-stress. No need to stay off social media totally, but try it for a little while, or for a few hours a week just link up online with close friends and family. Check out sites that make you feel happy and relaxed rather than worried and anxious. Arrange to meet up with friends in real life and go for a walk or just sit at home and chat or listen to music. This will give you the space to stop worrying.

WHAT IS ANXIETY?

Anxiety is when we are afraid, uneasy or worried about something unknown or uncertain.

DESCRIBING ANXIETY

Anxiety is the feeling of being worried or afraid of what might happen. It is feeling fearful of the unknown, of bad things happening, of the future. Physical symptoms include a racing heart, feeling faint, running to the loo, being tired and irritable, unable to sleep or concentrate, having bad dreams and losing your appetite.

As we've seen, these symptoms can be as a result of stress, and everyone will experience some of them at some time. But if you have symptoms like these for a week or so and they are affecting your schoolwork and stop you enjoying life, you should talk to a trusted adult. It might also help to see your doctor.

MAJOR CHANGES

Going to a new school when you move home or when you transfer from primary to secondary school is a huge change for young people and can make them feel very anxious. Try thinking about it as a new adventure. Yes, it is a bit scary, but in an exciting way. Be positive and open about what the new school holds and look forward to the challenge. If it all seems a bit overwhelming, talk to someone you trust or phone a helpline (see pages 46-47). It may not seem important enough to bother anyone, but if it is making you anxious and scared, then you should talk to someone about it.

BIG AND BAD

Sometimes, sadly, terrible things happen. Someone dies or becomes very ill, a family splits up or life changes in some way that is painful. When something this big happens we need to talk about our feelings, rather than bottling them up and putting on a brave face. It is perfectly okay and natural to feel sad and cry.

Sometimes a big life trauma can make us feel out of control and make us worry about other bad things that might happen in the future. This is natural and it will help to talk to someone about how you feel. Don't feel ashamed or embarrassed about feeling sad or afraid – it is completely normal to feel this way.

WHAT IF ...?

There are different forms of thinking that can make us feel stressed and anxious.

I CAN TELL THE FUTURE

No one can say what the future holds but that doesn't stop us worrying about what might happen. Some people who feel anxious think that the worst will happen, so they predict the exam will be an absolute failure, no one at the new school will like them and they will have a miserable life. Oh dear, that's a lot to worry about.

IT WILL BE AMAZING – OR AWFUL

This is when you convince yourself that the outcome of something will be either brilliant or a disaster. So the exam will be a total triumph or a complete failure. The pizza you're making will be the best ever or absolutely disgusting. The truth is, most things are never that extreme.

I KNOW WHAT PEOPLE THINK

This is when you think you know what people are thinking or are going to think about you. You know they will think you are stupid, laugh at your hair, hate your clothes and talk about you behind you back. You have no reason to think this, and everyone might be being very nice, but you have it stuck in your mind that this is what is going on.

THINK AGAIN

If you catch yourself thinking in any of these ways, stop and have a rethink. How do you know things will go badly? Is it really realistic to think in these extreme terms? And if you do fail the exam or your pizza isn't the best ever, is that really the end of the world? Even if things don't go as well as you had hoped, there will be other chances to try again and do better.

OVERTHINKING

Overthinking is when you think or obsess about all the tiny details of something non-stop, looking for different meanings or reasons. Or when you worry about small details after the event, such as what you said/should have said/didn't say/could have said. Argh! Social media can be particularly stressful as you worry about what to write, why no one's 'liked' you, whether you wrote the wrong thing, whether people misunderstood what you wrote, whether you should

rewrite it, on and on …

it's exhausting!

Stop, now!

Think about something else that is fun and positive. Read a book, listen to your favourite music, do some exercise. If you let your thoughts swirl about in your head, they will just go on and on making you feel more and more wound up, so make a choice to stop them and take control.

GOOD THINKING!

Everyone has times
when they think the world is
against them or that they
are useless, but you can
change the way you think.

HERE'S A SITUATION ...

Imagine you've taken a science test. Your teacher **says** you thought through the answers well, but unfortunately you failed the test because you got some facts wrong.

How would you feel?

A

It would have been good to pass but at least you got some positive feedback. You can do some extra research into the facts you didn't know.

B

You are useless at science and probably everything else as well.

If you chose B, you are forgetting or filtering out all the positive things people say about you and that you know about yourself. This is very common and lots of people do it. We remember the bad or negative things people say about us rather than the good, positive things. If you believe you are rubbish at science, that fact you failed the test will support this. You will forget that you actually did some good work in the test.

DON'T FORGET THE GOOD STUFF

When you start to have negative thoughts about yourself, take a deep breath, sit in a quiet space and think it through. Are you really that bad at science? If you are, why did your teacher say you gave some good answers? Think about how you can do better next time. Feel good that you got some positive feedback and make a plan to do better next time.

ONLINE SOCIAL STRESS

On social media you may get some nasty comments, or not enough comments or 'likes', or people may suddenly block you for no reason or leave you out of invites and messages. Don't think it is all your fault and that you must have done something wrong. People do things for reasons we don't always understand. Block the person that is upsetting you or switch off the blog that makes you feel bad about yourself. Your time on social media should be fun, creative and supportive.

TRY THIS!

Keep a diary or memory jar of all the positive and good things that happen to you – scoring a goal in football, mastering a dance move, someone giving you a compliment, suddenly understanding the maths problems, getting a good mark for your essay, making a new friend. When you feel negative or bad about yourself, take a look through your diary or pull out some memories from the jar and remember the positive things.

STRESS AT HOME

Your home should be a safe, happy place but every family has times when they go through a bad patch or difficult experiences.

FAMILY ARGUMENTS

All families have disagreements and arguments. Adults and children get cross with each other but they soon make it up. Sometimes, though, the arguments can get nasty, especially between adults. Perhaps rows get longer and louder, the adults throw things or even hurt each other. If this is happening in your home or you feel scared, anxious and unsafe there, you must tell a trusted adult. You are not telling tales; it is your right to feel safe. And sometimes, if another person steps in, it can help solve the problems that are causing the arguments.

NOT GOOD ENOUGH

Most parents and carers only want what is best for their children, but sometimes this means they push them to achieve the top results, to go to the best university or to excel at a subject such as maths or sport.

This puts a lot of pressure on young people to succeed to please their family. It can cause them added worry and anxiety, especially if they are not as successful as their parents would wish. If you feel this pressure, talk to the people it's coming from. Try and explain that you are doing your best. If it is the case, explain that the constant pressure of always having to succeed can make it difficult to sleep properly or concentrate on schoolwork, so it has the opposite effect.

FEELING SAFE

Your home should be a safe place and your family safe people to be with, but this isn't always the case. No matter how difficult life is at home, usually children continue to love their family and don't want to get them into trouble. But suffering high levels of stress and anxiety as a young person can affect someone for the rest of their life. Stress releases chemicals into the body that can can be linked to illness later in life.

Mentally, constant stress and worry can cause depression, feelings of worthlessness and isolation and lead to self-harm and even thoughts of suicide. If you are feeling threatened, anxious or scared at home you must speak to a trusted adult or phone a helpline (see pages 46-47).

MAKING FRIENDS

Social events should be
fun, but many people find they
make them feel stressed
and anxious.

MEETING NEW PEOPLE

Being anxious about meeting new people and being in
new situations is normal. Remember that most other
people are feeling the same as you. Smile, say "hi" and
be friendly. Listen to what people have to say and ask
questions without asking anything too personal. Keep in
mind that not everyone will instantly get on and become
best mates, and we can't be friends with everyone. If
you don't feel a connection with someone, don't force it
or change to try and fit in with other people.

DEEP BREATHS

Some people start to blush when they feel anxious. They
might even begin to sweat or stammer. This happens to
lots of people and is nothing to worry about. The more you
think about it the worse it will feel. You probably notice it
a lot more than anyone else. Take deep breaths before a
stressful situation, and be determined to make the best of
it, whether it's taking a test or joining a new club.

BEING JUDGED

Some people feel very anxious and scared about meeting new people or talking in front of a group because they believe that they are being judged. They think they will do something silly and make a fool of themselves and be laughed at. This makes them feel even more anxious and might stop them doing things such as joining new groups and clubs and making friends.

If you feel your anxiety about meeting new people or talking in front of a group is making you feel ill or stopping you making friends, you need to talk to someone you trust about it, either face-to-face or via a phone helpline. Feeling this way is nothing to be embarrassed about and it is not being silly. There are lots of ways that your doctor or specialists can help people overcome these feelings of anxiety.

HOW DO I LOOK?

Are you anxious about how you look or worried whether people will think you look okay and want to be your friend? Remember we can't all look and be the same.

You are you, a special and unique person and you don't need to change yourself to fit in with a group or crowd. Be friendly and kind to other people. Be proud of your own style and looks. Find friends who like you for who you are.

66

When a new dance class started locally I was really excited about joining. But when the day came I felt really anxious. I thought everyone else would be great dancers and I would make a fool of myself! Walking into the room my knees went to jelly and my heart started beating really fast. I almost turned around and left but felt determined to give it a try. I'm pleased I did. Everyone was very friendly and I'm loving learning the dance routines and making new friends.

Lina, 12

99

PANIC ATTACKS

Panic attacks can happen to anyone at any time, but what are they and why do they happen?

THE SIGNS OF A PANIC ATTACK

A person who is having a panic attack can experience breathlessness, a feeling that something terrible is going to happen, feeling sick, dizziness, a fast-beating heart, a feeling of choking and feeling very hot or very cold. An attack can be caused by a number of different things. If someone has had a panic attack they may get stressed about having another one.

WHY DO THEY HAPPEN?

Most people like to have a regular routine where they know what is going to happen and what is expected of them. When this routine changes, it can make us feel anxious. For young people there are lots of changes in life, such as starting new schools and making new friends. This can increase anxiety and worry, and trigger something like a panic attack.

AVOIDING ATTACKS

When someone has a panic attack, it is very natural for them to avoid doing whatever it was that caused the panic attack in the first place. So, whether it's going through a tunnel or joining a new group or club where you don't know anyone, the thought of doing those things again will be terrifying and the person will do everything possible to avoid them.

The best way to overcome the fear is to do the same thing again. You can do this with someone you trust. Or you can ask your doctor for specialist help. Remember no one dies from panic attacks and they do not mean that there is anything physically wrong with you.

TRY THIS!

If you ever have a panic attack, find an adult and tell them what is happening. Breathe slowly. Look at your favourite photos on your phone to take your mind off what is happening. Call a friend or family member, someone you trust, that you can talk to until you feel better. Panic attacks are very scary but they only last about ten minutes, although it can seem like forever if you're having one.

ROUTINES AND RITUALS

Everyone has little routines they do to help with stress, but sometimes these can grow to become an obsession.

WAYS OF COPING

When we are anxious or worried we do lots of little things to help us cope, and sometimes we don't even know we're doing them. For example, if you're going out for the day, your mum or dad might check more than once to make sure they've got the car keys or that the back door is locked, even though they already know the keys are in their bag and all the doors are safely locked! Maybe you hum, or tap a pencil, or count to 100 to cope when you are feeling stressed. These small routines are harmless and can be very soothing and reassuring in stressful situations.

KEEPING THE BAD AWAY

Sometimes these little routines or rituals can turn into an obsession. This is when a person feels they have to do them to stop something really bad happening. If they can't, they become scared and anxious, and might have signs of a panic attack. Sometimes this is called Obsessive Compulsive Disorder (OCD). Scientists don't really know yet what causes it.

HIDING THE FACTS

Young people who have irrational fears and behave in this way sometimes feel too embarrassed or ashamed to talk to anyone about it. They try to hide their rituals from friends and family in case they are teased or laughed at.

If you think you may have OCD or if your routines are stopping you doing things or upsetting your home or school life, you need to speak to your adults at home about it. There are lots of different ways that doctors can help with OCD so there is no need to suffer alone.

"

It started when I was 11. I became anxious that someone in my family would become really ill and I worried about germs killing us. I had to wash my hands all the time. I spent ages washing before bed and when I came home from being outside I would wash and rewash my hands and arms in case I brought germs into the house. Mum took me to see a doctor who understood why I felt so anxious. He suggested some therapy. You have to work out why you feel so anxious and find ways to control it. It's hard work but I'm much better now.

Jeffrey, 13

"

HELP AT HOME

If you're feeling anxious
or worried you need to talk to
people at home about it.

DON'T FEEL EMBARRASSED

You may feel embarrassed or silly talking to your parents or carers about your anxiety or worries. Maybe you feel that you should be able to cope, especially if you have siblings or friends who are managing school, homework, friends, joining clubs and passing exams. But everyone is different so don't feel that just because everyone else is coping, you should be able to as well.

We all need help sometimes and it is your parents' or carers' job to look after you and help you when things get difficult. It is very grown up to recognise that you need help and to ask for it. The sooner you ask for help the sooner you'll start to feel better.

WHERE TO START

Choose a quiet time to talk about your worries. Rather than saying something out of the blue over dinner or when they are rushing to get to work in the morning, tell your parents or carers you want to talk and ask them to set a time when they can give you their full attention. Everyone needs to be calm and focused, including you.

If talking face-to-face is making you feel more anxious, write your worries down in a letter and ask your parents or carers to read it when they have some quiet time.

BE TRUTHFUL

Be as honest as you can about how you feel. Explain that you feel anxious and it is making you feel sick and scared, or you worry all the time about being asked to read in front of the class or whatever it is that is troubling you. They may say that you'll grow out of it, or that it will get better, or to keep on trying.

If you feel your parents or carers don't fully understand, call a helpline (see pages 46-47) and ask for advice on how to speak to them or speak to a trusted family member or a teacher about how you feel.

> "
> *I spoke to my dad when I was feeling really anxious about giving a class talk. Just the thought was making me feel sick. Dad noticed that I was quiet and spent a lot of time in my room, so when he asked what was wrong, we sat down and had a chat. He understood more than I thought he would – said he used to feel anxious about talking in front of people as well. Just talking to him and knowing he understood really helped a lot.*
>
> Sam, 11
> "

ENJOY LIFE

A healthy diet, having fun, exercising and getting a good night's sleep will all help you to keep stress and anxiety under control.

GOOD DIET, FEEL GOOD

How you look after your body affects how you think and feel. Nutrients such as vitamins and minerals in fruit, vegetables, fish and carbohydrates help to keep your brain working and growing well. They help you to concentrate on your schoolwork and improve your memory, as well as helping you to cope with mood swings and feeling down. Eating too much sugary food will make you feel sluggish and slow physically and mentally. Keep sweet things as a special treat every now and then.

EXERCISE – IT WORKS!

Exercise releases chemicals called endorphins into your brain. These endorphins help to make you feel happy and good about yourself. When you do any exercise that makes your heart beat faster you pump more oxygen around your body. Oxygen keeps your brain in good working order and helps to keep you feeling alert. Exercise also keeps you fit so you feel good about your body. When you feel good physically, this helps you to cope with worries and anxiety.

ZZZZZ

A good night's sleep helps you to concentrate and cope with challenges. Not getting enough sleep can make you feel grumpy and not able to focus on schoolwork. Lack of sleep might also make you feel physically tired so you won't be able to play games as well as you might and you won't enjoy being with your friends as much as you usually do.

FRIENDS AND FAMILY

Being with good friends or family, having fun, chatting and laughing, reading a brilliant book or watching your favourite film, sharing your day with people you love and who care about you and doing activities that make you feel excited. All these things help you to feel relaxed and happy, and when you feel like this you are better able to cope with stress and anxiety.

You can also help friends and others who may be feeling anxious or stressed. Listening to other people's problems and being there to give them a hug will help them and make you feel good about yourself. Have fun, relax and enjoy yourself.

THE LAST WORD – POSITIVITY

You might have heard
a lot about positivity or
being positive, but what does
that mean exactly?

THROUGH GOOD AND BAD TIMES

No one feels bright and happy and fully in control of their life all the time. Everyone has times when they feel sad, anxious or stressed – that's perfectly normal. The idea is to learn how to cope with the bad times, and being positive can help with this.

Being positive is remembering that nothing bad lasts forever. No matter how sad or angry or anxious you feel, it can and will get better. The bad feelings may pass naturally with time, or you can ask for advice from a professional person or a helpline to help you through, but either way you can and will feel better.

POSITIVE THOUGHTS

Positive thinking can help everyone every day. If you have a difficult task ahead, such as an exam or a class talk, instead of imagining the worst will happen, think the best will happen: you will do well in the exam and make a great presentation. If it's not perfect that doesn't matter. The fact that you tried your best is what is important.

TRY THIS!

Start the day saying something positive, such as: "Today will be a good day." It will get you in the right state of mind for the rest of the day. And smile! Even if you don't feel like it, it can make you feel better. Give it a try!

GLOSSARY

BLUSH
when your skin, especially your face, goes red

CARERS
people who look after a child who are not their natural parents

COPE
to be able to deal with something

DEPRESSION
an illness that affects us physically (symptoms include not being able to sleep, always feeling tired, having no energy) and mentally (feeling anxious, tearful, hopeless and alone)

EMOTIONAL HEALTH
how you feel mentally, about yourself and the world around you

ENDORPHINS
hormones released into the brain and body that make us feel good

FEAR OF MISSING OUT (FOMO)
anxiety that you may miss an event, especially one that has been talked about on social media

HEALTHY DIET
eating the right sort of foods, such as lots of fruit and vegetables, bread and pasta, avoiding too much fast food or sugary food, and drinking plenty of water

HORMONES
chemicals made by the body that help it to work as it should

IRRITABLE
snappy and cross all the time

ISOLATION
being alone

MENTAL HEALTH
how you feel about yourself and the world around you, your moods and how you cope with life

MOOD SWINGS
quick changes in mood, such as feeling happy one minute and sad the next

OBSESSIVE COMPULSIVE DISORDER (OCD)
repeating activities more times than is needed, such as washing your hands over and over again and checking things repeatedly, such as if a door is locked

OVERTHINKING
thinking and analysing something too much in a way that is harmful to your mental health

PANIC ATTACK
a sudden and overwhelming feeling of fear that can cause a pounding heart, sweating and shaking

POSITIVITY
being positive and thinking things will get better and work out well

REASONING
thinking about something in a sensible and logical way

RITUALS
a series of actions with a special meaning

SELF-ESTEEM
confidence in your own worth and belief in yourself

SELF-HARM
hurting yourself deliberately, usually in secret

SIBLING
a brother or sister

SLUGGISH
slow and tired

SOCIAL MEDIA
websites and apps online that allow people to share information and keep in touch

STRESS
when you feel physically or mentally very tense or worried

SUICIDE
the act of killing yourself

UNIQUE
the only one in the world

VISUALISE
to create a picture of something in your head

WORTHLESSNESS
having no use or value

NOTES FOR TEACHERS, PARENTS AND CARERS

Here are some strategies for ways teachers, parents and carers can recognise mental health issues in children and how to help them.

TEACHERS

Signs of a stressed or anxious child include withdrawal; lack of concentration; repeated behaviours such as drumming, tapping and rearranging pencils, and reluctance to talk in class.

HOW YOU CAN HELP:

* Read through this book with the class and talk about stress and anxiety. Many children will feel they are the only ones suffering in this way and may be ashamed or embarrassed about it.

* Allocate a quiet stress-free room where children can go and sit and be quiet during non-lesson times. Invite students to think of this as a space where no worries are allowed, where they should think about nice things and have positive thoughts.

* Have a time when students can sit with a teacher to talk through their worries with them. Make this a private space.

* Have a worry box, a box somewhere private where students can post their worries anonymously and unidentifiably. Teachers can then talk about these worries in class or at assembly.

* If a child seems very anxious and it is affecting their school work, speak to the head teacher about contacting the parents or carers.

PARENTS AND CARERS

Signs of anxiety or stress in young people include becoming withdrawn; not doing things they would normally enjoy, such as seeing friends or playing sports; trouble sleeping; having bad dreams; being irritable; angry outbursts; lacking confidence and having difficulty concentrating.

HOW YOU CAN HELP:

* Talk to your child about how they are feeling. Explain what anxiety and stress are, as many children may not be able to name the feelings they are experiencing.

* When your child becomes anxious, ask them to talk to you so you can help them. Make sure they are aware you are listening to them carefully and are taking them seriously.

* Suggest your child keeps a book to write down all the things that makes them anxious or stressed. Read through the book with them after a certain length of time and see if the 'bad' thing happened or if, in fact, everything went better than expected. This might help your child to get their worries in perspective.

* Set aside a certain time each day to talk about what is worrying your child. This way the child knows they can "deal" with their worries at a certain time and gives them a sense of having control over the worries.

FURTHER INFORMATION

WEBSITES AND HELPLINES

If you feel overwhelmed by any of the issues you've read about in this book, or need advice, check out a website or call a helpline and talk to someone who will understand.

https://www.brainline.org/article/who-me-self-esteem-people-disabilities
How to boost self-esteem regardless of disabilities.

www.childline.org.uk/info-advice/your-feelings/mental-health
Message or call the 24-hour helpline for advice or someone who'll just listen.
The helpline number is 0800 1111.

https://kooth.com
Free online support from professionals, real-life experiences and a place to talk and write about your worries with people who understand.

https://www.nhs.uk/live-well
For advice on mental health, sleeping well and a healthy diet.

kidshealth.org/en/kids/feeling
Advice on managing emotions.

www.youngminds.org.uk
Advice for young people experiencing bullying, stress and mental or emotional anxieties.

www.samaritans.org
A place where anyone can go for advice and comfort. The helpline number is 116 123.

www.sane.org/get-help
Help and support for anyone affected by mental and emotional issues.
The helpline number is 0300 304 7000.

www.supportline.org.uk
A charity giving emotional support to young people.
The helpline number is 01708 765200.

FOR PARENTS AND CARERS

https://youngminds.org.uk/find-help/for-parents/parents-guide-to-support-a-z/parents-guide-to-support-anxiety/

AUSTRALIA AND NEW ZEALAND

https://kidshelpline.com.au
A helpline for young people giving advice, counselling and support.
The number is 1800 55 1800.

www.kidsline.org.nz
Helpline run by specially trained young volunteers to help kids and teens deal with troubling issues and problems.
The number is 0800 54 37 54.

Note to parents and teachers: every effort has been made by the Publishers to ensure that these websites are suitable for children, that they are of the highest educational value, and that they contain no inappropriate or offensive material. However, because of the nature of the Internet, it is impossible to guarantee that the contents of these sites will not be altered. We strongly advise that Internet access is supervised by a responsible adult.

BOOKS

Keep Your Cool:
How to Deal with Life's Worries and Stress
by Dr Aaron Balick, Franklin Watts, 2014

Dr Christian's Guide to You
by Dr Christian Jessen, Scholastic
Children's Books, 2016

Positively Teenage
by Nicola Morgan, Franklin Watts, 2018

INDEX

ISBN 978 1 4451 6451 9 (HB); 978 1 4451 6452 6 (PB)

* What is stress?
* Stress test
* Coping with stress
* What is anxiety?
* What if ...?
* Good thinking!
* Stress at home
* Making friends
* Panic attacks
* Routines and rituals
* Help at home
* Enjoy life
* The last word – positivity

ISBN 978 1 4451 6473 1 (HB); 978 1 4451 6474 8 (PB)

* Social media, it's great, right?
* Social media and your brain
* Oh, no! FOMO!
* Exclusion zone
* Please like me!
* Not real life
* Body image
* Developing self-worth
* Cyberbullying
* Sleep well
* Online help
* Take a tech break
* The last word – selfies!

ISBN 978 1 4451 6471 7 (HB); 978 1 4451 6472 4 (PB)

* Dream team!
* Hello, brain!
* Hormone havoc!
* Eat well
* Issues with eating
* Self-esteem
* Body image
* Sweet dreams!
* Always tired
* What's so good about exercise?
* Be positive!
* A healthy future
* The last word – mindfulness

ISBN 978 1 4451 6469 4 (HB); 978 1 4451 6470 0 (PB)

* What are emotions?
* Emotional chaos
* What else affects moods?
* Emotions and thoughts
* Emotions and behaviour
* Sweaty palms and a red face!
* Feeling sad
* Feeling happy
* Feeling angry
* Feeling scared
* Relationships
* Friends for life
* The last word – me!